A Kaleidoscope of Thoughts

A Kaleidoscope of Thoughts

BY

Syed Ibrahim Rizvi

GenNext Publication

First Published, 2020

Published by

GenNext Publication
5, Ansari Road
Daryaganj, New Delhi-110002
Phone: 9811692060
E-mail: gennextpublication@hotmail.com

Printed at: G. Print Process, Delhi.

Cataloging in Publication Data—DK
Courtesy: D.K. Agencies (P) Ltd. <docinfo@dkagencies.com>

Rizvi, Syed Ibrahim, author.
A kaleidescope of thoughts / by Syed Ibrahim Rizvi.
pages cm
ISBN 9789353242459

1. Life. 2. Thought and thinking. I. Title.

LCC BD431.R59 2020 | DDC 128 23

Dedication

This book is dedicated to my father Late Agha Rizvi who through his genes gave me the gift of weaving thoughts into words

Contents

Preface

Thoughts have no boundaries. This book is a compilation of random thought sequences which has been documented at different time intervals in the form of short articles.

A few articles focus on the various aspects of life. Indeed human life is amazing. Animals also have a life but humans have an aspect of intellect coupled to being living creatures. The human intellect creates infinite possibilities which are manifested through endless emotions. The beauty of life lies in these emotions.

Some of the articles bring forth the nuances of human behaviour. Why memories give us joy? How telling a lie is inherent to our behaviour, and what is the genesis of romantic love?

The author acknowledges the bias towards biology and the evolutionary process in some of the articles. It is indeed highly interesting to view life through a historical perspective spanning 4.5 billon years since life originated on this earth.

Overall the book is intended to offer interesting articles for a discerning audience having an interest in English language.

Syed Ibrahim Rizvi

Acknowledgement

For the last thirty years I have literally lived with Biochemistry. All my academic pursuits till now have focussed on biochemistry research and teaching, however, somewhere deep in my brain there always lurked the passion for creative writing. This compilation of short essays is a beginning of the expression of life's desires which have not yet found a vent. Through this endeavour, I acknowledge the contribution of the dedicated teachers of my first school, the Boys High School, Allahabad who took pains to instil in me the nuances of English language.

Chapter - 1

Living a happy life is a self prerogative

While debate can continue, the best possible parameter to assess the quality of life is the degree of happiness that one perceives. Life in its full journey passes through a series of different age-dependent zones all requiring a new definition of happiness.

As easy as it sounds, finding a barometer to quantify happiness is a difficult preposition. The changing goal of life as one moves from childhood to adult and then into the twilight zone makes it deceptive to quantify the paradigm of happiness.

It is interesting to note that something which makes us happy at a given moment in life may become a reason of distress at another point of time. The joy of bunking classes, skipping homework and being lazy to school during the initial years of life suddenly become a reason for stress a few years down the life's journey.

In today's materialistic world, wealth may seem to be a major contributor to the happiness quotient. This notion may indeed be true for those who have limited wealth but those with a fair amount of wealth may disagree. In most cases, it is the wealth which becomes the cause of stress in life.

Success is another parameter which may contribute to a sense of happiness. While success is indeed a potent elixir, its achievement is mired through a path which is mostly through stressful hiccups. Success is also strongly associated with a sense of ambition. The same ambition which leads to success may also become a cause for depression.

The best possible definition for happiness in life could be a situation with a least amount of stress. This definition of happiness has the best chance to survive the changing moods of life from childhood to adult and then to the old age.

While happiness is difficult to define, stress is almost impossible to explain. Any situation which goes against the accepted norm of the concerned individual elicits a set of physiological and biochemical response in the body which takes the form of 'stress'.

Biologists broadly explain the condition of stress in terms of secretion of certain chemical substances in the body known as hormones. The most potent and active hormone released during stress is the hormone called cortisol. While the biological importance of this hormone lies in its role of preparing the body for an adverse situation, its continued secretion is highly detrimental.

Any situation in life, be it the travail of a child coping to complete homework, the teenager preparing under peer pressure for board exam, the tryst with a lost love, the endless applications and the subsequent regrets from employers, the comparison of the salary which always seems to be on the lower side, the impression of wife which seems to be less beautiful than someone else's, and children not doing as expected.....the list is endless, is associated with increased secretion of cortisol inside the body.

Every time the release of cortisol (the steroid hormone) is more than the requirement; the body goes into stress and loses some amount of joy which is the essential ingredient of happiness.

Nature has made every human being unique. The great diversity in human race mimics the diversity in wealth, success, resources, environment, and many other parameters which cumulatively define happiness. Thus for every individual the quotient of happiness is unique. It is our response to stress which gives the best idea whether we are happy or otherwise.

Life is a nature's gift which is too precious. After all we live only once. Although we have no control where we are born and what are the inherent conditions, to live life to the fullest is certainly our own prerogative. While everything comes with a price, happiness can be achieved simply by limiting the level of stress.

Chapter - 2

The beauty of life lies in its uncertainty

In the beginning there was nothing....... (Genesis 1.1)

The earth and the moon and the sun would not have been so beautiful if there was no life on earth. To this day, despite intense scientific explorations, there is no other place in this universe where life exists, at least in the form in which it exists on this blue planet.

In the historical perspective of our earth, perhaps the greatest milestone stands 3.7 billion years back when the first primitive molecules chanced to interact with themselves creating a self replicating structure which was the beginning of life. Our minds are not tuned to fathom the eons which might have passed while the earliest lifeless molecules created almost infinite combinations before life could originate in the form of a nucleic acid molecule.

The sheer time frame of history of life on earth is mind boggling. We as humans have a lifespan of around 80 years which is so tiny a fraction to the time scale of life that even an effort to understand the enormity would lead to mental chaos. If the history of life can be depicted by a hundred kilometer long road then humans have a lifespan of only Two millimeter!

While scientists still grapple with the events which might have happened leading to origin of life, the only thing which can be said with a fair amount of certainty is that the process was highly uncertain. Paradoxically even after 3.7 billion years, with evolutionary forces creating a huge kaleidoscope of diverse life forms, life has retained its basic instinct. It remains highly uncertain!!

Current biological knowledge prides itself in understanding the anatomy, physiology, biochemistry and psychology of living creatures. The molecular events which act in concert to maintain the approximately 40 trillion cells in our body making us living creatures are extremely organised and act with great fidelity.

Thus in the backdrop of highly organised life structure of all living organisms, why is life so uncertain in its lifespan? Would life have been better if there was no uncertainty associated with its course? This situation would have made it easier to predict the future course of events in one's life. However, choosing a path of one's own life without the fear of failure or going astray would have created a situation of eating your favourite food three times a day all the year.

The beauty of life lies is the twists and turns that it offers from childhood to old age. The sense of achievement when a goal is fulfilled is a feeling which brings immense joy. It is in this labyrinth of glorious uncertainties which life offers lies the joys, sorrows, expectations, aspirations, fears and surprises. All of these combine to make life such a beautiful experience.

The beauty of the essence of life's challenges has been very aptly described by the famous Urdu poet **Asghar Gondwi**

Chala jaata hun hansta khelta mauj-e-havadis se
Agar aasaniyan hon zindagi dushwar ho jaa-e

It is indeed a sad feeling when humans do not value this immensely unique natural gift which we define as 'life'. After all we live only once. Life in itself offers us a huge array of pleasant moments and difficult times. It sometimes throws challenges which are unforeseen and seemingly difficult. Indeed there is absolutely no scope for man made events such as violence, war, hatred, and malice.

Chapter - 3

What is the purpose of life?

All living organisms take birth, grow, live for a certain amount of time, and then die. Although this path is common to all living creatures and almost universal, nature doesnÕt provide a specific answer to the question: What is the purpose of life?

Human beings have been around for approximately 200,000 years on this earth. Although 200,000 years is a small timeframe with respect to the time since the origin of life which is about 3.5 billion years, it still is a big enough span for evolution to work on creating an intellect which has made possible the large knowledge base and intelligence that we possess.

Despite huge advances in science, humans have not yet been able to find any mechanism to extend life span beyond the maximum limit of 122 years. Not only for humans, all animals have a definite lifespan. Thus, in all its pristine glory, if lifespan had to be finite then there must be a valid reason why life has survived the vagaries of time beginning with the origin of life some 3.5 billion years back.

At every point in the evolutionary history of living organisms there must have been events which could have threatened the very existence of life. The fact that living systems survived all potential catastrophic exigencies provide enough evidence to suggest that indeed life should have a paramount purpose.

The answer to this vexed question depends on infinite choice of interpretations based on factors as varied as religion, culture, philosophy, or belief. Scientists believe that the sole purpose of life is to ensure continuity or in other words to ensure reproduction. This scientific basis is backed by large credible evidence of robust systems in all life forms for mechanisms to ensure propagation of progeny.

This explanation also provides an answer to another biological paradox: why do we age? If everything goes by logic then eating good food and living in better conditions should promote youthfulness rather than cause aging and eventual death.

Gerontologists opine that any living organism when it accomplishes its essential purpose of life, which is reproduction, is no longer required by nature and from this point onward there is a gradual decline in body functions which we define as aging. Till the attainment of age at which an organism is expected to reproduce, nature provides it with a warranty period.

It is a common observation that all degenerative diseases in humans manifest after a certain age which is just after the time when youth merges with middle age.

It is thus not without reason that everything associated with the essential purpose of life, which is reproduction, is so pleasurable. Romantic love, a prelude to a possible reproductive event, is perhaps the most pleasurable of all human emotions. Recent scientific evidence show that even in fishes which precede humans by almost 1.3 billion years in the evolutionary time scale, there is some form of pleasure associated with a sexual event.

Notwithstanding the purely biological explanation of our existance, human endeavours have far exceeded the confines of natural logic. The plethora of artistic creativity, the almost exponential rate of scientific discoveries, the fast changing sporting milestones, and a new thinking process have changed the paradigm. Humans as a race have now almost overcome the pressure of evolution.

Despite the intellectual abilities which now define humans, there are situations when the primitive basic instincts takeover the thinking process of our brains. The 200,000 years of our existence as humans is too short a time span to shed off some of the inherent basic instincts of survival. This explains why some of us resort to certain acts which in the civilized society are now classified as crime.

Chapter - 4

Romantic love and human survival

The origin of life on earth started a sequence of event which is still continuing. Amazing it is that from an earliest life form which could have been just a few biomolecules, the journey of life has travelled unabated for 4.5 billion years creating the huge variety of life forms which presently inhabit the earth.

The self sustenance of life through these billions of years is certainly a nature's marvel. No one knows the origin and mechanisms which compelled early organisms to engage in sexual activity leading to reproduction and production of off springs. The driving force of reproduction has rather been instinctive during most periods of evolutionary history. The biological link between the reproductive act and pleasure is perhaps a recent event in evolution and possibly unique to humans.

Among all living creatures, humans are unique to have evolved a mechanism of pair bonding among individuals through a very beautiful emotion classified as 'romantic love'. No other creature on this earth displays this kind of pair bonding.

The act of existing as mates for an extended time, even beyond the successful completion of reproduction, owes its origin to the requirement of the male to help the female partner in taking care of the newborn child. The first instance of such behaviour becomes evident just a few million years back coinciding with the time of evolution of humans from chimpanzees.

In all other animals, the care of the newborn is always a burden on the mother. The concept of father came only with the advent of humans. The most important biological necessity which prompted a paternal link to child care in humans, compared to other animals, was the increase in the size of the brain of the new born.

The increased cranial size also required that the gestation period be shortened considering the requirements of foetal development. Thus the human newborn is most underdeveloped amongst all animals. No other animal baby requires to be taught to walk or swim.

In chimpanzees and other primates, which are close to humans in the evolutionary scale, there is a strong prevalence of infanticide or killing of the baby by the male in an effort to gain access to the female for sexual mating.

Thus the development of the emotion of romantic love created a condition which promoted bonding between mates and ensured that the male of the bonding pair also contributed to the infant care. Scientists believe that romantic love emanated from the ingrained animal instinct of love between the mother and child.

In its foremost instinct to ensure continuity of life, nature has devised its own indomitable strategies. All facets of living organisms, which are important for survival, have been linked to some form of pleasure. Eating good food, adequate work/rest, sex, sleep, and a host of other activities which in some way enhance our chance of healthy living, are associated with a feeling of pleasure. It is thus not without reason that nature has bestowed the emotion of romantic love with the highest amount of pleasure which anyone can experience.

The emotion of romantic love not only creates a mating relationship which is favourable to the survival of the newborn but has also been instrumental in the shift towards monogamous relationship from the polygamous instinct of our nearest primate relatives.

Despite all attributes, genetic and ethical, romantic love in its most basic format always tries to create a situation conducive for a reproductive event, the all important prerequisite for life to sustain. Reproductive event once accomplished, the biological need of romantic love no longer exists. Is this the reason why husbands are affectionate to their wives but cannot be romantic after marriage?

Chapter - 5

Nature's design: Perfectly imperfect!

In all their endeavours humans have always tried to achieve perfection. This all persuasive instinct has constantly played a stellar part in driving human civilization forward.

Can anything be perfect? The answer to this question is difficult. Perfection is a relative term and is an adjective which only emphasizes the relationship of any condition in comparison to an existing arrangement. Thus one can only aspire to be perfect, achieving perfection is not possible!

Every innovation is a perfect example of mankind beating its own created paradigm in an effort to attain the elusive state of perfection. The zest for perfection thus continues to propel scientists, architects, sportspersons, painters, sculptors, musicians, and exponents of all forms of arts in improving their performance. A false sense of having achieved the ultimate would stall human progress and would be extremely detrimental.

The discovery of new and next generation antibiotics from the early days of discovery of penicillin in 1928 by Alexander Fleming, constant improvement in the production of vaccines for a host of human diseases, creation of architectural marvels from the early designs based on arches and domes, and the breaking of athletic records and sports milestones are but a few examples of human instinct trying to achieve perfection without actually achieving it!

Although the quest of being perfect may be elusive in human achievements, there are physical conditions and laws which are always perfect. The laws of physics have no scope to be imperfect. Avagadro's number, Plank's constant, and the speed of light is just a tiny example of physical events which are never imperfect. The perfection and the fidelity of physical laws are astonishing.

While the pursuit of perfection has propelled human civilization, biological structure of life has thrived on the fact that it has always been imperfect. The imperfection of the molecular structure of living creatures has made life sustain its journey through changing environmental conditions all through the long expanse of its history spanning 4 billion years.

The DNA which is the most important molecule in living systems needs to replicate itself (make an exact copy of itself) before any cell can divide and growth can take place. This process is same in all living forms on earth from the lowly bacteria to humans. Nature has bestowed all living systems with 'perfect' machinery to make duplicate copies of DNA ensuring that the progeny receives the same DNA which was present in the parent.

The beauty of seemingly 'perfect' design of nature is that even the process of duplication of DNA is sometimes 'imperfect'. While the property of 'perfect' duplication is so essential for life to sustain, the 'imperfection' which happens approximately once in a billion DNA duplication events has been instrumental in creation of immense diversity of life forms on earth.

The 'imperfection' of DNA duplication results in a condition known as mutation and forms the basis of Charles Darwin's famous Natural Selection theory explaining the creation of new species.

The inherent imperfection of the molecular logic of life has perhaps also cast a shadow on our thinking process. Our concept of beauty, one of the most basic instincts, is perhaps dictated by our choice of acknowledging 'imperfectness' as a defining feature rather than the state of being 'perfect'. Most beautiful human faces have a large amount of vertical a symmetry. Would legendary Rekha be that beautiful if she had a vertically symmetrical face?

The beauty of the subtle kink in Madhubala's smile and the mole on Cindy Crawford's face highlight the importance of 'imperfectness' in nature's design.

Chapter - 6

Can we live without telling a lie?

Deceit is a crime when used in human relationships. The instinct of creating an alibi in certain situations of life is a common feature in almost all cultures. The universality of being knowingly untrue either in spoken word or action is probably the genesis of the phenomenon of telling a lie.

Since the advent of civilisation, there is historical evidence of humans using this seemingly innocuous trait of speaking a lie for reasons which are too innumerable to define. It has thus been of no consequence that all religions have preached against the use of lie. As time passed and humans created their own laws and constitutions, it emerged that there are laws for all human aberrations except for speaking a lie! It is only when one speaks a lie on oath that it is considered unlawful and amounts to perjury.

Although despised in all societies, there is probably no human who can for certainty muster the courage of stating that he/she has never spoken a lie. Indeed if there is a soul so pure, it could only be an angel in disguise. The joy of speaking a lie is too ingrained in our system.

The use of lie being imperative, one is constrained to think whether it has its origin in our DNA. However, there is no scientific evidence for the existence of any gene which codes for our instinct to speak a lie.

Although no parent would inculcate the habit of telling a lie to their children, it emerges that among the earliest playful instincts which the child displays is the art of lying. A child hiding a toy to the gleeful gaze of parents is a sight to behold. A toddler knowingly denying eating a chocolate, a child pretending to be sick just to escape going to school, a student offering a false excuse for not completing homework, an adolescent coming home late, and an employee seeking leave for a reason not true are some of the situations where we have started using a lie almost as a law!

The famous evolutionary biologist Theodosius Dobzhansky said "Nothing in Biology Makes Sense Except in the Light of Evolution". If speaking a lie is so universal and a natural instinct which does not require to be taught, there should be some evolutionary benefit for its use. It is indeed conceivable that speaking a lie in certain situations may have benefits which outweigh the virtues of being truthful. Even the concept of humour is based on situations being incongruous or inconsistent with reality.

Despite the universal human instinct to use lie as a scapegoat in numerous everyday situations, there are instances when the virtue of being true has been awe inspiring. The story of Baba Bharti admonishing the thief of his cherished horse not to mention how he tricked Baba and stole the horse, still continues to inspire school children.

Although lacking in the skill of language, animals also frequently resort to situations which is akin to the human concept of speaking a lie. Many species of animals use camouflage to escape predators. Some even pretend to be dead when faced with a non escapable situation banking on the ego of the predator that it will not eat a dead animal!

Although one is not certain how to classify the art of telling a lie and whether it is a necessity or an evil. It is indeed hard to envision a society sans the use of lie; it constitutes an essential repertoire for a professional politician and a survival tool for a cheating husband.

Chapter - 7

When 'dil' and 'jigar' became synonymous

Not with standing the likes of great thinkers and philosophers such as Mohammad Iqbal and Faiz Ahmad Faiz, Urdu poetry is strongly linked to matters of love and romance. In fact as a language, Urdu stands high on the pedestal of poetry. The art of expressing thoughts in couplets (Sher) is perhaps unique in linguistic domain.

Bollywood songs have always been a fertile ground for exponents of Urdu poetry to showcase their talent and in the process earn a living. The art of Urdu poetry which blossomed in the times of later Mughals was always in penury. Even greats such as Mirza Ghalib found it hard to make a living.

With the advent of movies, Urdu poets who could capture the romantic imagination of masses were much in demand. The romance portrayed on the screen of bollywood movies was frequently accentuated with imaginative and hyperbolic poetry weaved into melodies created by equally talented music directors. It was in this era of Indian movies beginning from early 1950's that songs personifying some high class duets of poetry and music were created.

The advent of bollywood music and the need for songs in movies primarily as a medium to express love, narrowed the realm of the Urdu language to the description of romance and love. However even this parochial requirement could not restrain highly talented poets and song writers to find innovative ways for description of various aspects of love.

It was in these creative endeavours that poets exemplified heart as the seat of emotions. Defying biological principles, the heart became the totem of love in poetry. Perhaps the poets described heart as the prime seat of emotion because this organ was the best example of life in the living organism.

Other than the heart, bollywood poets used eyes, hair (zulf), face, lips, and other features of anatomy profusely in their songs to conjure up images which soared the imagination of a conservative society. The simile with moon and the darkness of night were often used by exponents of poetry to accentuate the canvass of romantic environment.

In their quest for imaginative ways to provide romantic thoughts, sometimes the poets went overboard in their descriptions. While the heart as the site of love may be explained as a poetic liberty, one finds it hard to explain the usage of 'jigar' (liver) in matters of love! It thus goes to the credit of song writers who used 'jigar' in such convincing style that many would start ascribing liver to be linked to romantic thoughts.

It is difficult to forget the sight of an utterly beautiful Nutan dumbstruck to the serenading Shekhar lip-syncing to the melodious Mohd Rafi song 'Tujhe kya sunao mein dilruba...' in the 1958 movie Aakhri Dao. Majrooh Sultanpuri used the lyrics ' mere dil jigar mein saman bhi jaa, rahe kyun nazar ka bhi faasla' (my beloved.....integrate into my heart and liver, why should there be some distance, even in sight). The use of the word 'jigar' was so ingeniously crafted that it could pair with 'dil' without any subjugation.

Even after 70 years, the song is as romantically iconic as it was in 1958. Hats off to Majrooh sahib for using a piece of human anatomy, which has nothing to do with love, as an object of love chemistry.

Chapter - 8

Friendship: A unique human trait

Humans compared to other animals have a large lifespan. Despite this ‘achievement’, life in its true sense is too short! Humans are different from all other animals because of their intellect. The ability to think, reason, understand, and apply this to useful work leading to inventions and productivity are the hallmarks which make humans unique among all living creations.

The evolutionary forces which played important role in development of human race, also made humans a creative species designed to work in social groups. While several animals display strong social behaviour, humans evolved a specific attribute which made them choose other individuals based on likes and dislikes. The criterion of friendship thus was born from this evolutionary attribute.

It is said that while we cannot choose our relatives, we can choose our friends. So what makes us choose our friends ? Life offers a huge array of personality traits which makes all humans unique. Finding a friend would thus have to do something with these traits. Do we look for similar traits? or compatibility? or there is some other mechanism?

While scientists and evolutionary biologists may debate about what we look for in a ‘friendship’, the bottom line is that this is perhaps the most ‘beautiful’ relationship known to mankind, which is unparalleled to any other bonding or attraction. This relationship is not challenged by age, sex, caste, religion, or any other divisive force which life can throw.

Interestingly the same forces which play their part in finding a friend also become important in mate selection. Thus this characteristic of humans also has a strong evolutionary advantage. Possibly this could explain how humans evolved to become monogamous from the polygamous animal instinct.

The idea of finding solace in someone else's company is perhaps the best definition of friendship. Interestingly this bond imbibes within itself an immensely pleasurable emotion of giving and sharing which is not replicated otherwise in relationships which are a result of common genetic inheritance.

Friendships which start from childhood are usually qualified to be included in the true sense of this immensely strong bond. Later life friends may or may not display all the inherent characteristics of this association. Professional friends usually are friends for the namesake. The common ground is the work place rather the elements which define friendship.

History is replete with instances where friendships have shaped course of civilizations. The institution of friendship is such a strong element of human nature that losing a friend is perhaps one of the most depressing events. It is indeed dreadful to even think what would have happened if evolution would not have given humans such a lovely instinct. Life would have been a one long arduous task if there were no friends. It is only our interaction with 'friends' which make us finally realize: life is too short!

Chapter - 9

Transition of moon from a simile to metaphor

The transformation from four legged stance to bipedal locomotion was one of the biggest events in human evolutionary history. Not only this event created a new way of walking but also made the hands free for gesticulation. The art of conveying information to others with gestures of hand and face was the beginning of language.

As time passed the origins of language became apparent. The common evolutionary instinct of language can be understood from the nearly universal roots of grammar in all languages known to humans. The use of 'motherese' or baby talk, which is the use of distinct speech patterns and vocabulary when talking to young children, in all human cultures and linguistic domains, is a testimony to the common origins of all major languages.

It is almost a recent event in evolutionary timescale that humans have developed mental faculty wherein the art of communication, both vocal and written, has taken the form of exhaustive language and vocabulary.

The earliest human evidence of language skill involved poetic forms of expression. The ancient works, from the Vedas (1700 - 1200 BC) to the Homer's Odyssey (800 - 675 BC), appear to have been composed in poetic form. Perhaps the poetic expression aided in memorization and oral transmission.

Poets and writers for ages, in their artistic pursuits, have used different forms of expression to mesmerise audiences into surreal thoughts using farfetched but captivating similes and metaphors.

Of all the objects used as similes that have formed part of the repertoire of poets and linguistic artists, the moon has by far eclipsed all expressions. From a forlorn object of romance, the moon has frequently been used as a measure of beauty. The comparison of the moon to the beloved has been a favourite romantic thought in so many poetic expressions that even the moon may have lost count of it!

A full moon on many occasions has also been referred to as an intruder in romantic settings. The sight of Nargis wishing for the moon to look the other way while she sings *Dam Bhar Jo Udhar Munh Phere* in the milestone Raj Kapoor movie *Awara*, has nothing to implicate the moon for its beauty or as a simile with the beloved.

In different settings, the beautiful reference of 'moon' as a metaphor has created perfect romantic situations. The use of 'moon' as an object of recommendation in the song *Chand sifarish jo karta....* from Amir Khan's *Fanaa* is as enchanting as is the melody of this beautiful song.

The use of moon as an object of celestial distance and remote destination has also been very eloquently used in the Meena Kumari lip synced song *chalo dildar chalo chand ke paar chalo* in Kamal Amrohi's classic *Pakeezah*.

Its iconic romanticism notwithstanding, the moon's fairy tale image conjures up a childhood memory in every adult human. The universal 'chanda mama' still remains a Pandora box of fond memories much to the delight of children.

The impressive biodata of moon, wherein the similes and metaphors sometimes camouflage its celestial importance, is perhaps incomplete without reference to its importance during Karwa Chauth when the viewing of the full moon by married woman ensures safety and longevity of the husband. Interestingly while its appearance marks the start of festivities during Eid, the expression 'Eid ka chand' refers to a long-lost friend.

While humans have used the existence of moon and its lexicon for their own worldly benefits, few have cared about the travails of the moon itself. Only once did moon speak and that too through the pen of noted hindi poet Ram Dhari Singh Dinkar in the poem 'Chanda mama'. Who can forget the moon's request to his mother for a pullower to tide over winter's cold nights!.

Chapter - 10

Indian ethos and opulence

The Indian civilization, apart from being the oldest in the world, also prides itself for being a cradle of numerous customs and traditions which are innately humane.

The 'gurukul' system of education, the respect of the elderly, the joint family concept, and the respect of woman are virtues which are ethnically Indian.

An integral part of Indian way of living has always been the preference of a modest lifestyle over something extravagant. In situations where extravagance became necessary, it has never been considered a virtue but always considered something alien.

Is it therefore a sign of cultural erosion or insensitivity that Indians are lapping a lifestyle which is far removed from the traditional Indian ethos?

The opulence of recent high profile marriages has put to shame the real India. The blatant display of wealth is a silent offender to millions of Indians who have no means to get two meals a day. The abject surrender of the high and the mighty who willingly chose to serve meals at such functions highlight the change in society where money can buy not only material things but also the status of superstars.

The media has also contributed to the process of deterioration of Indian traditional culture and values. The extreme fascination of the media to the fancy events related to Priyanka-Jonas, Deepika-Ranveer, and Sonam-Anand marriages is in total contrast to the values which make India such a great country. These are characters created by the fantasy world and cannot be the role models of millions of youngsters who will take our nation forward in years to come.

The real Indian heroes can be found in the village farms, busy streets, middle class homes, government schools, forlorn borders, and lonely hospitals.

A farmer toiling in the field to make his daughter complete school, the government servant working tirelessly without joy only to pay fee for his son's IIT education, a woman at home doing menial jobs only to save money for her daughter's marriage, a father who cycles 20 kilometer to take his son to a cricket academy, and a young boy who swims across the river to reach school are the real Indian heroes! While India ushers in 2019, lets salute these unknown individuals who contribute to the nation building.

Indian culture is rich in values when it comes to the institution of marriage. Across religions, marriages in India are always solemn occasions. The concept of someone else's tattoo on the nape and husband's mangalsutra on the neck is definitely alien to our society.

Chapter - 11

The perception of time: Real or illusion

Perhaps the most valuable ingredient in our lives is 'time'. Its importance from the moment of birth to death is absolutely essential. The whole lifespan is but a timeline of events happening in a linear forward direction chronicled in minutes/hours/days/months/year.

It may sound unreal but documentation of 'time', in the form that we perceive, is a recent creation owing its evolution to the ingenuity of humans. The beginning of 'time' on earth owes its origin to the circadian rotation of this planet on its axis creating a unique sequence of day and night. The fixed duration of the circadian motion provides a tool to calibrate its length into defined periods that constitute the 24 hour day.

The moon also provides, through its own revolution around the earth, a regular event which can form the basis of calibration of 'time'.

Beyond the solar system, 'time' may not exist in the form that we recognize. All those places in the vast universe where there is no rhythmic or recurrent event may lack a scale which can be calibrated to make a calendar. Thus the 24 hour clock which we follow on earth is probably unique to our planet. Even the closest celestial object, the moon has a different time scale. One moon-day is 28.5 Earth-days long!

The concept of time on earth being based on its rotation and the system of day and night that follows, is depended on the sun and its light. Had there been no light in the sun, the earth would have rotated and revolved but no visible circadian difference between day and night would have happened. Thus 'time' owes its origin to light.

It is therefore not without scientific fact that the speed of light is a precise measure of duration of time and in the process a suitable scale of distance. The dependence of time to light also proves why nothing can travel faster than the speed of light. 'Time' certainly cannot overtake its own genesis, the light!

The history of time on earth is approx 4.6 billion years. The human recorded history is too small and thus in our perception 'time' remains a constant parameter. It may sound mind blowing to know that that in the infancy of solar system the earth's rotation was much faster and it took only Seven hours to complete the day/night cycle.

Scaling the passing of time has always been an endeavour for mankind. Time measurement dates to approximately 2000 BC in Egypt where the Sumerians used sundials or shadow clocks to calibrate days into smaller units of time. The sands of time are thus witness to the instruments from the days of 'hourglass' to modern day precision watches which have helped humans to keep pace with 'time'. At present a second is equal to Nine billion oscillations of the caesium atom.

Interestingly the concept of time is also a major attribute that differentiates humans from other animals. Although animals exhibit circadian events and resultant behaviour, there circadian changes are dictated by environmental cues like sunlight, darkness, temperature, pressure, wind speed and direction, seasons, and availability of food. A sudden darkness that ensues during a solar eclipse is a powerful trigger for birds to come to their nest.

According to Einstein, time is relative, flexible and an illusion. Indeed illusion it is. The same duration of time that seems endless for a sick is a fleeting moment for two lovers at a rendezvous. Paradoxically, a virtual entity which has no real existence, time offers an endless variety of linguistic expressions in all known human forms of communication. It can be good or bad, hard or pleasurable. The metaphors our endless.

Chapter - 12

When a 'no' means 'yes'

No other living creature on earth except humans display the unique ability of effective communication based on a system of vocal expressions which constitutes a language. Evolutionary biologists predict the timescale of evolution of language in human history around Two million years back.

Language, as we recognise in its present form, is a very recent creation in human history timescale. The origin of language dates back to a long period of time when communication was confined to gesticulation using hands and facial expressions. Interestingly the presence of eyebrows on our faces has been explained on their use by primitive human ancestors as a means of communication when oral language skills were not developed!

Although around 7000 languages are presently spoken in the world and the use of words are infinite, perhaps the most common word used in all languages is 'yes'. It is the symbol of affirmation, acceptance, and agreement. The power of 'yes' is undeniable. The almost universal tradition of handshake is based on the evolutionary basic instinct of conveying affirmation which signifies the feeling of agreement or 'yes'.

The power of 'yes' is again exemplified in another universal tradition, the art of greeting based on the use of 'good morning'. What a better way to start a communication beginning with something which is agreeable to both communicators!

The power of the word 'yes' finds use in yet another human behaviour, the expression of showing respect. A subordinate answering a phone call of an officer, a student responding to the attendance call of a class teacher, a soldier responding to the briefing of his officer, and a sales man trying to impress a buyer, all use the innocuous yet powerful expression: 'yes sir'.

The evolutionary instinct of using a sign of agreement or affirmation, which is now exemplified in our spoken language as the word 'yes', finds ample use in situations where basic instinct takes over the articulation and confines of language. The sight of Jasprit Bumrah pumping his hand in the air after taking a wicket, Ronaldo running towards the crowd after scoring a goal, and Roger Federer exulting after a powerful forehand, all these basic emotions come with the universal exuberance of the powerful-'yes'.

The universality of the importance of the word 'yes' is not complete unless one takes into account the meaning and usage of its antonym, the equally powerful,' no'. Although being on the opposite side of the same coin, the use of 'no' is slightly difficult. A 'no' usually signifies disagreement, inability or a lack of certain attribute. The use of 'no' is more a sign of despair or helplessness.

An interesting difference between the importance and usage of the words 'yes' and 'no' is that while a 'yes' always means yes, the 'no' can have different meanings. An emphatic 'no' is much different than a passive 'no'.

Curious is the case of a passive 'no'. Its meaning sometimes changes to 'yes' in human interactions. Take the example of a typical Indian guest, when confronted with the mundane question whether he would like to have a cup of tea, the answer is invariably a passive 'no', however in such situations the meaning of 'no' is always taken as a 'yes' by the host!.

Sometimes the use of 'no' gives more pleasure than a 'yes'. The sweet use of a 'no' in romantic situations by the beloved is far more exciting than a blatant 'yes'. Who can forget the iconic song of Rajesh Khanna – Farida Jalal starrer Aradhana in which the hero asks different questions which have answers in the affirmative and the last question being: '*tumko mujhse pyar hai*' ? The sight of Farida Jalal saying 'na na na' still remains romantically iconic. Here the 'no' definitely means a 'yes'.

Chapter - 13

Media controls how and what we think

Our thinking process is a result of complex brain functions which are influenced by the information we receive from the environment. Thus the thinking process is not an independent action but depends upon the information which is given to the brain.

In its most basic form the nature comprising of living organisms, plants, seasons, and natural environment influence our thoughts. However, in recent times the virtual environment comprising television, internet and the resultant social media, have greatly influenced how we think and what we think.

The constant intrusion of information through technology has created a situation where our mind has become a hostage of media. We no longer live in a condition of free thought. The media tells us what is to be watched and what must be believed.

In this media controlled atmosphere the identity of a person is lost and everyone becomes a clone with a similar thought process. Marketing companies hypnotise our senses making us believe into a materialistic world. Political parties create media campaigns which play into the minds of unsuspecting population.

The psychological impact of media driven human thought process is huge. Books and all sources of authentic information are becoming obsolete. It is the 'google' and 'yahoo' which have become knowledge banks without any guarantee of what is correct or incorrect.

The dividing line between what is real and what is virtual has blurred to an extent that we now talk of 'virtual reality'. The huge technological advancement in the area of computer driven image creation has made the brain a virtual hostage of what is shown. The evolutionary neuronal circuitry of the human brain which creates perceptions based on perceived information has been successfully deceived by virtual reality.

Thus, although technology has made our life so easy, we unknowingly have paid a huge price. Our thoughts and emotions are not our own, we now live in the age where emotions are no longer expressed by a laughter or a tear, the new mantra is a junk of 'emojis' which give vent to our expressions. The intrusion of media has also created paradigms such as the concept of 'fake news'.

Thus we now live in a virtual world where even the absolute 'reality' is 'virtual'. Times are changing fast, days are not far when a media 'hypnotised' society would cease to have any independent thought. Gone will be the days when it was said 'seeing is believing'.

Chapter - 14

How to deal with memories

Life follows a winding journey which is full of joy, sorrow, apprehension, desire, contentment and a host of other emotions. In this exciting journey some moments stand out which subconsciously become etched in our minds. These defining moments of life standing out as milestones, become memories which remain with us for our life.

Some of these memories which are unpleasant create a kind of load on our minds. Recalling these memories later in life brings forth the same unpleasantness which in the first place became the genesis. These memories are difficult to erase and are buried deep inside the brain. With the passage of time they fade in intensity but are never erased. Perhaps this is a mechanism of the mind to remind us of things which may not be repeated.

The memories which stand out and become a cause to cherish are the ones which have an element of joy or happiness. The mind continues to play these memories recreating the happiness these memories once stood for. In John Keats words " A thing of beauty is a joy for ever: Its loveliness increases; it will never Pass into nothingness; but still will keep". So apty described.

The joy associated with recalling the happy memories sometimes becomes even more intense when the memories are so personal that they cannot be shared. They remain vaulted in the confines of our brains, cherished and valued. It is a difficult question how we deal with such memories.

A possibility is that we treat them as a bunch of gas balloons. They give immense joy when they float at some distance tied to a string, dancing to the invisible tune of the slow moving wind. However, keeping them for long does not guarantee continued happiness. The best option is to release them before they lose their strength to fly. The flying balloons in the clear sky, merrily wafting among the clouds, provide a perfect epilogue to the joys of the memory they once stood for.

Some may however argue against the idea of letting your fond memories fade away with time. After all memories are there to be enjoyed and cherished. Thus can fond memories be looked upon as vintage postage stamps? Pasted on the envelopes the stamps act as engines of loving messages being transported in the post. However job once accomplished, the stamps become part of a philatelist delight. Just as fond memories sitting in the recess of our minds, these stamps find space in the album growing in importance with the passage of time.

One may therefore have different opinions how we deal with pleasant memories but no one can deny the fact that the joy of recalling a fond memory is worth a million smiles. William Wordsworth said "For oft, when on my couch I lie, In vacant or in pensive mood, They flash upon that inward eye Which is the bliss of solitude; And then my heart with pleasure fills, And dances with the daffodils"

Chapter - 15

In times of choices galore, peace of mind takes a hit

Human journey on this earth has witnessed great revolution. From the days of cave dwellers to our present day habitat, the path has been highlighted by scientific achievements wherein our choices have tremendously increased. The time has come to analyse how the option of choice affects our present day life.

People in their 50's and 60's would still fondly remember the days when sitting before a black/white television screen with the revolving Doordarshan logo accompanied by a vintage slow motion tune, was a pleasurable experience. The programmes which followed, including a 30 minute 'Chaupal' for farmers, were viewed with so much intensity that even the call of nature would be postponed till the last.

The joy of watching 'Doordarshan', with the frequent intermittent blackouts, was a pleasurable experience only because there was no alternative available. The mind was always at peace and therefore the content dished out on the flickering B/W bulging screen TV sets was so enjoyable.

As time passed and technology overtook the thinking capacity of the human mind, in a short span of three decades, there are infinite choices as far as content available on the TV can be counted. Although the choice is almost mind boggling, is the mind at peace? The surfeit of channels provides more stress than joy. One is always under the impression that there can be something better on another channel.

The plethora of choice has even contributed to dismantling of the hierarchical setup of the traditional Indian household. With TV channels dishing out entertainment for every age group, there is always a latent fight between the different generations of the household for the TV remote.

The curse of the choice becomes even more interesting is several other man made situations. Not long ago, a happy moment for the quintessential Indian middle class family involved a visit to a pizza joint. Usually it was the birthdays or a happy event which would trigger a celebration when the head of the family would open his purse for eating out.

Eating a pizza with melted cheese on the bread base not only satisfied the palate but also made a status statement next day in the school classroom.

Times have changed. Today a visit to a pizza joint is always associated with more stress than joy. The range of choice displayed on the board is in itself frightening. One is made to choose from regular/medium/ large. Once done, the offer of a deluge of toppings with varied price tags forces the mind imagine every option before deciding.

The travail gets harder when presented with the choice of type of crust: stuffed, thin, crispy, multigrain etc. A few more questions down the line are enough to cause depression. Finally the options for the accompanying drink leads to exasperation.

The joy of eating a pizza has now become a curse only because of the number of choices.

Would life have been better if the number of choices available to us were less? An answer to this vexed question can only be possible if we consider that the chaos of available choices is man made. Science tells us that for anything to happen spontaneously, the entropy of the system must increase. Entropy is the technical term for 'chaos'. Thus for life to progress, it is important that chaos must increase.

The night sky looks beautiful only when the stars appear in chaotic disarray creating infinite illusions. Even the romance of the clouds is due to their boundless aberrations. No wonder our life's journey is also no less than a chaos!

Is it not worth wondering whether the apocryphal Chinese curse *May you live in interesting times*, is actually true?

Chapter - 16

Sacrifice: Thy name is woman

God created Adam from the dust and then to make his companion, he created Eve from one of the ribs of Adam. So goes the narrative in the Book of Genesis of the Bible. Thus even in God's design, Eve played second fiddle to Adam. The Biblical narrative further goes to explain how the serpent deceived Eve to taste the fruit of the forbidden tree leading to the banishment of Adam and Eve from the Garden of Eden.

Religious perspectives may sound hyperbolic, but pure scientific knowledge also lend credence to the fact that even biologically there are many differences between males and females. All inherent qualities of females in some way complement the existence of man. After bestowing male with strength, dominance, power and arrogance, nature compensated its folly by complimenting female with beauty, compassion, love and humility.

Perhaps it was in acknowledgement of the prime qualities bestowed upon the female sex that nature entrusted the responsibility of propagation of life to the weaker sex. The genesis and continuation of life on this earth owes its existence to females of all animal species. The sustenance of the difficult gestation period and the childbirth is a huge sacrifice which the female makes for mankind.

The evolution of humans through a 3.5 billion years of historical process created intellect and intelligence hitherto unparalleled with any existing animal, however, the development of patriarchal society brought certain concepts which were beyond logical explanation. Humans became the only species which started discrimination against female sex. A large section of the society still does not celebrate the birth of a girl child.

From childhood, the girl learns to play second fiddle to her younger or elder brother. Specific instances apart, the child herself is not able to recognize how her status is always a notch below the boy in the household. The situation is so rampant that nobody understands the emotional sacrifice of the girl.

A few years past the childhood, the girl undergoes another societal diktat for wearing clothes which conform to the parameters of a particular cultural group. The girl is made to make another sacrifice. While the male is free to make merry, the girl is wrapped into boundaries of customs and traditions.

The Adolescent and teenage girl is probably the most vulnerable person in a family. While biological development creates a myriad of psychological uncertainties, the social pressures are overbearing. The emotional sacrifice of the girl is lost in the chorus of family norms and traditions. For the male child the teenage years are full of joy and tantrums, the girl in the family is frequently made aware of her future responsibilities.

The youth is a period when the female is expected to look beautiful. Nature has also provided her with the instinct of accentuating her looks for the mundane reason of eliciting the attention of a prospective mate. While in principle the thought of cultivating beauty may look pleasurable, the constant need to fulfil this elusive attribute is indeed a big sacrifice.

It is thus a paradox that the male in the patriarchal society looks for such cues in the female which were always a taboo during the early life phase of the girl. A girl, in most cases by compulsion, is encouraged to look desirable for a prospective mate.

Nature's design of reproduction once accomplished, the female is required to change roles. From an object of desire she takes the mantle of motherhood which has a totally different definition. The frequently changing roles of the female are always associated with extreme sacrifices which even she is unaware.

It is indeed a sad commentary that we do not acknowledge the supreme sacrifice of the gender which transforms itself from a girl to a sister to a wife and to a mother without making us aware of the inherent sacrifices involved.

Chapter - 17

How the game of cricket lost its 'Gentleman' tag

The primitive animal instinct of dominance was necessary for evolutionary process because it ensured that the best suited individual got a better chance of reproduction.

The evolution of humans brought the saner side of human intellect into fore. Societies evolved wherein the animal instinct of dominance by force became unlawful. It was in this backdrop that different sports came into existence. This advent of sports provided a channel to express the inherited animal instinct of dominance based on brute strength.

It is thus not a mere coincidence that all major sports have some element of combativeness based on strength and skill. The use of strength and skill in almost all sporting events is aimed at expressing dominance. Essentially all sports end with a winner and a vanquished.

Indeed curious is the case of game of cricket which owes its origin in England sometime in the 16th century. Perhaps cricket is the only sporting activity which has such elaborate rules and laws. Its laws are not only confined to elaborately defining the playing conditions, they also bring into their ambit the kind of emotions which the players must display!

The laboriously crafted laws and bylaws have left no scope for the players to indulge into any emotional exuberance which might give a faint glimpse of the animal instinct of dominance. It therefore was a unique concept that the game was played more for the skill rather than for winning or losing. Since cricket in its approach epitomised the highest form of human civilized behaviour, it became to be aptly referred to as the 'Gentleman's Game'.

The 150 years of test cricket has been testimony of the fact that even without the overt charm for winning, the game of cricket can be as fascinating to the players as well as to the connoisseurs sitting in the stands. Test matches ending in draw have sometimes provided more joy that those finishing with a result.

Cricket is perhaps the only sport where a ball going past the batsman, who has offered no stroke, and landing in the safe gloves of the wicketkeeper is a joyful sight for spectators, applauded for the 'well left' technique.

Who can forget the swagger of Clive Lyold, the lazy elegance of David Gower, the poetry in motion of Micheal Holding running in to bowl, the geometric precision of Sunil Gavaskar cover drive, the burly Farokh Engineer behind the stumps, Bishen Singh Bedi making the ball dance to his tunes, and Bhagwat Chandrashekhar twirling his wrist and making the ball turn foxing not only the batsman but also the wicket keeper. Cricket is thus oddly remembered more by things not actually related to the basic sporting action.

The pressures of modern society and the advent of television brought about a change in the game of cricket which took away the soul of the game. The shorter formats of the game brought the excitement in the game by virtue of creating a winner and a loser.

With money pouring in for the players and the crowd resembling the spectators in a Roman amphitheatre, the game has now become a virtual slam bang. A shot that a few decades back would be described by legendary Richie Benaud as 'lemon cut' and despised by spectators with a deafening silence is now applauded for the runs that it accrues.

In the din of glitz and glitter, white ball, coloured clothing, LED and neon billboards, infinite camera angles, and the staggering use of computers, the game of cricket has definitely marched with the times but has lost its sober innocence. The high octane bat-n-ball contests now on display, marketed by media as the game of cricket, is far removed from the ethos of the sport which was affectionately called – The Gentleman's Game.

Chapter - 18

How fictional thought shapes human lives

Even animals communicate, however their communication is limited to signals which indicate general environmental cues, prey, danger or mating opportunity. One to one communication started with the advent of humans.

The art of communication and weaving thoughts into verbal and gesticulated actions is perhaps the hallmark of *Homo sapiens*. The ability to express one's thoughts, relate the past with the present and the future, and even fantasize created a new dimension of human behaviour and so started the art of story telling.

With the advent of effective communication, humans started creating social groups much beyond the periphery of their immediate family and friends. This became the beginning of imaginary and virtual networks. In this virtual labyrinth of humans, the binding factor was a virtual entity whose existence was only fictional.

The present day idea of companies is an example of large number of unrelated individuals bound together not by any physical means but only by an ideology which has no real existence.

The common thread of imaginative thinking and fictional thought helped to bring diverse people together into large communities. This was the genesis of religious groups, castes, creed, race, and national identities. After all nations are just geographical creations. The line which divides two nations has no physical existence. Thus two sets of populations on either side of the border have separate imaginary identities despite the fact that they share the same weather, climate, water, resources and even the same language.

Within religions, the idea of different castes is also based on virtual boundaries. A logical thinking would bring out the grave fallacy of categorising a particular individual in a particular caste based on his/her ancestral name. Despite the biological logic, the idea of caste finds deep rooted instinct.

Manchester United, Real Madrid, Liverpool and Mohan Bagan are just virtual entities. Neither the governing body of these clubs, the coach, nor their players have any relationship with the existence of each of these iconic clubs. It is thus a paradox that fans around the world show deep allegiance to these clubs which are only fictional names and have no physical existence.

Back home, the whole idea of IPL is based on the instinct of humans to idolize the virtual entities which are marketed in the form of clubs. After all Mumbai Indians and Kolkata Knight Riders have no real existence. A player donning the colours of one team this year may play for the rival team next year. Would IPL matches be as interesting if teams are not given names but only identified as Team A or B?

The evolutionary instinct of human mind to weave imaginary thoughts and create illusions is also used by political parties to sway voters into believing a particular narrative. A critical analysis would reveal that political thought is only an imaginary state of the mind. However it is this fictional thought process that becomes a glue to bind millions into a virtual group of people constituting a political party.

The love of the human mind to derive pleasure from virtual entities is probably best exemplified by the popularity and the universal appeal of movies. Even knowing that what is being played out on the screen is but a non-existent virtual visual sequence, the human mind is happy to be deceived.

We are so different from other animals because humans have the mind for creative thinking. Animals view world only in the present tense. Our power to fantasize and create virtual entities has added a new dimension to our existence. Pure biological logic sometimes does not provide answers to evolved human behaviour. The art of fantasizing is perhaps unique to humans and evokes unforeseen joys.

Chapter - 19

Facial beauty: Ethereal innocence and hidden cues

A beautiful face is perhaps the most pleasing sight one may encounter. This observation leads to a question whether beauty is a universal attribute or as the saying goes 'it lies in the eyes of the beholder'?

A beautiful face in indeed a nature's gift and a result of approximately 2,00,000 years of evolution, the time since we have been on this earth as 'humans'. The characteristics of beauty, intricately camouflaged into the geometry of the human face, convey a lot more than what is visible to the eye.

The 'beauty' in the structure of face is perhaps the biggest indicator of good health and fertility when viewed in the light of mate selection. Beyond the ethereal innocence of a youthful face, hidden in the arrangement of nose, eyes, lips, eyebrows, chin, and cheekbone are powerful indicators which convey to the prospective mate all the information required for selection.

The human brain also developed during evolution intricate mechanisms to decipher the clues provided by the face matrix of the other sex. To ensure the synchronisation of this highly evolved behaviour, the perception of beauty was linked with the reward centre of the brain.

The reward centre of the brain is activated by activities which have some role to play in survival. Once activated the reward centre of the brain produces chemicals which act on other parts of the brain and provide us the feeling of pleasure. Perception of beauty is a powerful activator of the reward centre. Indeed, the adage " A thing of beauty is a joy forever" is based on this scientific principle.

Although both males and females generally agree on the overall parameters of attractiveness, nature has provided each sex with certain specialized perception attributes which search for clues important for selection of prospective opposite sex partner. Masculine facial characters visible to females include good health, honesty and cooperativeness. Males look for femininity in female faces which is perhaps a clue for fertility.

Despite such elaborate mechanisms articulated by the nature's evolutionary machinery aimed at ensuring proper mate selection, humans designed their own way to bypass evolutionary design. Some cultures adopted a mechanism of mate selection based on the concept of arranged marriage. More often than not, the initial selection was not dictated by natural instincts of mates but by the choices made by parents, mostly the females.

In this 'arranged' model of mate selection, nature's design got entangled with human desire of wealth, status and many other choices. It was in this cultural adulterated mate selection procedure, marriages happened but evolution did not progress.

'Love marriages' as the name suggests are not exactly 'love' marriages. This is an expression of the nature's way of finding the best mates based on facial beauty cues which signify a host of attributes recognized only by opposite sex mates.

While human evolution for most part of its 2,00,000 years history has progressed by mixing of genes between two mates dictated by natural processes of mate selection, recent attitudes in mate selection have seriously dented the importance of facial beauty. Unfortunately the attraction quotient is now provided by other parts of the body in a more blatant manner than what nature had envisaged.

Gone are the days when Mohd Rafi sang the Madan Mohan melody "**main nigahen tere chehre se hataon kaise**" in 1964 movie AAPKI PARCHAIYAN

Indeed in present times the 'chehra' or the face is no more an adorable symbol of beauty. The brazen display of body has shifted the focus from the subtle cues present on the face to the desire evoking lust. Is this the sign of changing times or have we compromised with our morals?

Chapter - 20

Is human life too short?

Every living organism on this earth has a definite lifespan. Scientists have still not fully understood why different animals have varying lifespan despite the fact that most animals have similar physiology, body composition, and biochemistry.

It is indeed very curious that among similar sized animals, humans enjoy a very large lifespan. Our similar sized animals have a lifespan of around 40-45 years.

Although bestowed with a large lifespan which is around 80 years, humans are always inquisitive to find ways to live longer. Biologists have different views on whether the human desire to increase lifespan may be possible or not. The dominant view is that our lifespan is a result of a million years of evolution, thus to expect this to change is perhaps too preposterous.

An optimistic view however hopes that, given the pace of technology which is too fast in the present times, interventions may be available in near future which will provide avenues for humans to achieve much longer life span.

Some decades back, life was perhaps less lucrative in terms of its course from birth to death. The stages of life were more or less clearly defined. The toddler was distinctly different from the child, the span of time between being a teenager to a youth was a care free period with almost no worries and pressure, advent of youth was without the constant pressure of competitive exams, finding a life partner was a job effortlessly executed by the parents, and old age meant playing with grandchildren. Even death was easy without the trauma of a stay in an ICU or on a ventilator.

The last few decades have brought almost an exponential change in the way we, as humans, live our lives. Perhaps this period has been the most defining moment of human existence. The advent of internet has almost totally transformed the way humans spend their time. Evolution did not in any way prime us to be sedentary creatures communicating with virtual entities in a setting where the distinction between reality and virtual was almost invisible.

The toddler, the child, the youth, the adult, and the old all are now on the same 'platform'. As a result, the young have lost their innocence and old have lost their respect.

The blud geoning rise in population and the fierce competition for available resources have added to the pressures of modern society. Gone are the days when summer vacations were a time to visit grandparents. The modern lifestyle doesn't allow any such luxuries, the summer vacation is now a synonym for coaching classes and intense preparation.

The fast pace of life wherein time seems to fly and the lifespan go past in a flash is very aptly summed up by these few lines of Gulzar sahib's poetry: ***Ab to din raat pe hi aake rukta hai.... Mujhe yaad hai pehle ek sham bhi hua karti thi.***

Thus, in present times, we as humans have perhaps now 'challenged' the evolutionary design of our increased lifespan. The average lifespan of approx 80 years now looks grossly inadequate. Life indeed has become too short.

What would happen if humans suddenly get a gift of time and have an ensured life span which is double to our present lifespan of around 80 years? A Faustian bargain? On the face of it a 160 years of life may appear an exciting proposition, but would this be as beautiful as it sounds?

The urge to do things in a time frame would suddenly vanish. Human endeavour would not be as enthusiastic as it is today. The joy of keeping pace with the time may change to a trudge with slow moving time.

Limited time has perhaps been the most positive catalyst for human race in its advancement in science and human creativity. There is always a joy in things which have an ending. Would love stories evoke the same excitement if they continue to go on without an end? The hundred metre race looks breathtaking only when it ends at the finishing line. Subconsciously even death, with its inherent fear, has a charm. An abnormally long life may limit the fear associated with death.

A longer human life span may also impact our lives in many other ways. The tunnel of time which provides a ray of hope to the depressed may become longer. Suicides would increase. A large lifespan without subsequent increase in reproductive timeframe may see several generations under one roof. The meaning of 'generation gap' would indeed need to be reinvented. Lastly, the idea of spending an extended period of time with their soul mates may not be a romantic thought for many.

Chapter - 21

When rain plays cupid

Indeed our earth is unique! Despite intensive explorations and scientific scrutiny, there is no evidence of any celestial body in this vast universe where life is present in the form that we perceive.

The earth's uniqueness is not only limited to its capacity to sustain life, the rotation and revolution of earth creates a system which makes possible the circadian day/night and the changing of the seasons.

The tilting of the axis of rotation and the revolution around the sun following an orbit which is slightly oval creates a situation which leads to changes in seasons during one complete yearly cycle of 365 days.

The change of seasons is a major contributor to a large number of life events in all living species. Seasonal variations lead to changes in availability of food, natural resources, reproductive events, health parameters and a host of alterations which make an impact on the quality of life.

While seasons change in all parts of the earth, the importance of the change in season is distinct in different parts of the planet providing a unique cultural identity to that part of the world. Western countries with predominantly cold climate rejoice with the advent of spring. It signifies happiness, energy and excitement. The phrase 'spring in the step' derives its origin to the qualities associated with season of spring.

While autumn is celebrated in Indian sub continent, its meaning changes drastically in western habitats. Autumn being a prelude to the prolonged harsh winters is looked upon in a gloomy scenario. No wonder the English expression 'autumn of life' refers to the later part of life.

While world remains obsessed with winter, summer, spring and autumn, curious is the case of monsoon in Indian sub continent. The advent of rains after months of scorching summer is a delight which few would hazard to ignore.

The first rains on the parched mud not only soothe the temperature but also creates an 'earthy' smell which is unique and so pleasant. Within a couple of days tiny grass sprout from the once lifeless land as if the first rains were enriched with some magical properties.

The first rains also elicit emotional exuberance in humans. From the dry and dull summer, the advent of rains is a big omen for romance. Poets and writers have profusely used 'sawan' the first month of the monsoon as a time when love is in the air. Innumerable songs in bollywood have been created where rains have added glamour to romantic relationships.

It is not only the rains which provide romantic joy to forlorn hearts, even the drops of rains have been used by poets to accentuate emotional relationships. The sound of rain drops have been frequently used in poetry as a synonym of romance evoking stimulus.

The evergreen song "*rimjhim gire sawan.....*" playing in the background while a lanky Amitabh Bachchan and a bubbly Maushmi Chatterjee drench themselves in rain at Marine drive in the bollywood movie 'Manzil' is a beautiful example how rains and romance are so closely associated.

Not only the rains, even the clouds in the sky present some interesting thoughts during the monsoon. The dark looming clouds, which otherwise would signify something negative, present a new meaning during the early monsoon. The dark clouds flowing in the sky alongwith moisture laden winds bring hope and expectation.

The joy of rains is perhaps inherent to our genesis. It is the presence of water which is responsible for life to flourish on earth. However to understand how cupid strikes during monsoon one has to experience the feeling of love.

Chapter - 22

How melody in bollywood songs died a slow death

There is no clear evidence of the evolutionary origin of music. Biologists opine that the roots of music can be traced to human history dating back before the advent of spoken language.

The universal appeal of music certainly certifies to its importance and the evolutionary benefits of this sound structure based on interplay of notes. It is indeed exciting to know that despite the different origins of music in different parts of the world, every musical structure is based on common twelve notes.

Scientists explain that the universality of the musical notes, despite varied origins, is due to the ability of the human brain to identify certain sequential variation in sound frequencies capable of exciting the reward centre of the brain and evoking a sense of pleasure.

Certain sequences of musical notes which are related to each other in a specified ratio create a sound which we classify as melody. The same notes put into a different sequence may be jarring to the ear and far removed from any melodious definition.

The Indian classical music based on 'sargam' has great similarity with the Western classical system which uses *do re mi fa so la ti do* as musical scale. Indeed music has no language and certainly no geographical boundaries.

Music in its purely native structure probably evolved as a cue to signify a state of happiness within a group of individuals. When language was not evolved, this was a means to communicate personal happiness among other individuals in the community. Although millions of years have passed since the time primitive humans used music as an element of happiness sharing, we still harbour this instinct in the present times. Happy occasions in our present culture are usually associated with loud display of music. Common is the observation that one tends to increase the volume of music, much beyond what is required, when a favourite song happens to play out.

Given the evolutionary association between happiness and music, it was no wonder that music got incorporated as an essential ingredient in all human endeavours where the aim was to create something pleasurable. As soon as technology provided the required opportunity to mix visuals with sound, music became an inseparable part of movies. It was therefore not surprising that earlier movies had an overdose of songs which was perhaps a strategy to fulfil the pleasure quotient of the story telling.

With technology enhancing the quality of visual treat of movies, music also transformed with the evolution of instrumentation. The second half of the twentieth century witnessed an era when music was used in the movies to enhance the pleasure quotient on the basis of its inherent melody. This was a time when watching a movie was limited to theatres and the melodious songs were played out on radio and transistors.

To sustain their musical appeal it was important that the songs of this era were adorable to the ears. The music directors created melodies which left an imprint on the mind through unforgettable tunes. Melodious songs were never at the mercy of the reputation of the actors who lip-synced them or to the locales used for filming.

As time passed, new technology brought television, video recorders and then computers. Watching a movie was not confined to theatres and moved to the comfort of the bedroom. While this transition was a welcome development, the role of songs in the movies suddenly took a metamorphic turn. The song in the movie was now not an audible element but became a visual treat.

In this new paradigm, there was no pressure on the music directors to burn midnight oil into creating melodies. The onus to make the songs pleasurable was now the prerogative of creative song directors who created such visual sequences on screen which compensated for the loss of melody in songs. The vulgar display of body and the emphasis on evoking lust has created a situation where the present day songs are no longer the musical treat of yester years.

The slow death of melody has encouraged many new forms of audio structures which are being marketed as songs. The style of repetitive stammer of unrelated words coupled with animated wavering of hands and fingers is now classified as 'rap' and frequently used in films. While some may find this style of expression somewhat pleasurable, purists can never forget the lilting melodies of Naushad, Shankar-Jaikishan, Madan Mohan, Laxmikant-Pyarelal and a host of others who have left a golden treasure of immortal songs.

Chapter - 23

Beyond its playful side, sports have evolutionary importance

If indeed there was any rule in the jungle, it is 'might is right'. Strength and dominance are the defining features of the constitution of law in the wild. The emergence of humans from the legions of animals brought a new attribute based on higher intellect. The new thought process of humans created laws which provided equal opportunities even to the weak.

Despite the emergence of social structure based on 'civilised behaviour' in human societies, the basic instinct of 'dominance' and 'show of strength' remained ingrained in humans, albeit at a level much below what is seen in animal behaviour.

The need to dominate in a societal structure became pervasive since this attribute provided early humans a strategy to enhance reproductive success. Strength and power became essential tools for mate selection.

As human race progressed and society evolved, the basic human instinct of dominance found a way to express in the evolution of various forms of sports. No wonder the earliest forms of sporting activities involved competitions based on human prowess of display of strength.

Running and combat sports such as wrestling were one of the first 'sporting' activities which evolved wherein individuals professed their exhibition of strength without any apparent harmful intent.

In the advent of sports, humans thus found an outlet to express their legacy of animal instinct based on 'might is right'. Sporting activities provided a perfect platform to attain social status since all such events were based on the concept of winning and losing.

It is debatable as to when exactly human behaviour veered from the 'animal instinct' to the earliest form of sporting activity; however the importance of sporting activities in human evolution cannot be underestimated. Early Greek history finds mention of tales of Gods where human strength was put to test in different situations. The Greek myth of legendary Hercules diverting the course of two rivers so that they flowed through the stables of King Augeas, continues to be used as a phrase for extreme human endeavour.

The importance of sports as a means of expression of human accomplishment is exemplified by the advent of Olympic Games in the ancient Greece which continued unabated from the 8th century BC to the 4th century AD. Such was the aura and the importance of the ancient Olympic Games that even war came to a standstill when the time came for the Olympic Games.

Although the Olympic movement could not survive a long period in history, the world never looked back in the progress of different sports whose ambit became much larger from the earliest endurance and combat disciplines. Few events in history can compete with the resurgence of the first modern Olympic Games in 1896 by the efforts of the Frenchman Baron Pierre de Coubertin.

The importance of sports became even more influential as humans entered modern times. With the creation of fully civilised societies and elaborate laws, sporting events became the only medium for the display of strength, dominance and superiority.

Although all modern sports thrive on the adage that the important thing is not to win, but to take part; the reality of sports in present times is perhaps far removed.

The basic instinct which is part of our inheritance load from pre-human behaviour is far more persuasive than the civilized adage. All sporting events provide the thrill, to the players as well as the audience, only when the resolve is to win.

In the long history of sports the focus has always been on its playful phenotype, we have certainly missed its unique importance as a medium of civilized human rivalry. Beyond what is visible to the eye with respect to exciting moments, wins, losses, and heartbreaks, sporting activities provide much more to human development than anything else.

Chapter - 24

Love is not time's fool

It is indeed a quirk of destiny that the evolutionary process created humans. Difficult it is to believe, but the fact is that humans represent only one twig of the huge tree created by the evolutionary process. There are unfathomable organisms that are more, or perhaps equally, evolved than humans.

Not with standing this paradoxically mundane nature of our existence, humans display some beautiful emotions which make them unique in the kaleidoscope of life forms on this earth.

The evolution of love as an emotion is probably the most precious gift that humans received when nature wired their brains. The emotion of love, as we perceive today, is an instinct which is too recent in the evolutionary timescale dating back to about a few million years.

No other creature on earth except the great apes display the kind of behaviour which can be classified as love. It is now established that the emotion of love emanates from an area of brain called the angular gyrus which has been developed quite recently in the evolutionary timescale, perhaps a few million years. This is also the area of the brain which processes the complex aspects of language such as the use of metaphors.

Against popular belief, the necessity for the evolution of emotional love was not reproduction but a tool for survival. Humans, as animals, were not endowed with any mechanism for fighting or defence. There was no brutal strength, no claws, canines, or fangs. The tool to survive was probably the ability to create bonds between members of the community. The ability to bond with each other was facilitated by the evolution of brain which provided mechanisms to perform complex tasks including elaborate communication skill and expression of emotions. Interestingly human offspring has the biggest brain compared to any other animal.

As time passed, the emotion of love became an instrument of pair bonding and the association of mates leading to reproduction. However the use of love for creating a situation for mates to reproduce is a recent phenomenon, probably hundred years or so. For a major part of human history, most marriages have been dictated for the sake of survival. The institution of marriage was a purely economic arrangement aimed at promoting survival and prosperity of extended families.

It is thus not surprising that romantic love was not an accepted means of pair bonding or marriage just a couple of centuries back. Despite nature instilling the higher order of brain development wherein romantic love was already linked to reward centre and the release of love chemicals, dopamine and oxytocin, the society despised the notion of two individuals loving each other and pledging to stay in association.

The romantic tales of Romeo-Juliet and Laila-Majnu are testimony to their defiance of accepted societal norms in moments of trance when biological force of love chemicals overwhelmed their rational thinking. The reason why present day history does not create such romantic heroes is because the society has now accepted the notion of romantic love as a prelude to marriage.

The basic instinct of love was also a ploy by natural selection to create a situation in which two mates get an opportunity to be in extended association for a successful reproductive event. This was also a starting point for monogamous behaviour, a deviation from the predominant polygamous behaviour of animals.

Being a natural creation, love is perhaps the most innocent and pure human emotion. It is also conceivably the most pleasurable experience known to humans. The same romantic love which becomes a prelude to reproduction is modified to a condition which leads to companionship after the need to reproduce is diminished. Couples staying together in an obsessive companionship bond for an extended period owe their association to release of the hormone oxytocin.

While the instinct of mate selection evolved rather separately than the emotion of love, the two got aligned at some point of time in our history. Thus love being an overriding emotion for humans; it has frequently surpassed the pleasure of mating and the inherent process of mate selection. This biological observation has been beautifully summed up by Shakespeare when he wrote 'Love is not time's fool," in sonnet 116.

Human life without romantic love would indeed be extremely bland resembling a piping hot soup without salt. By its sheer sublimity, no other emotion comes close to matching the pleasure of being in love. Or why else all romantic stories would end with lovers becoming soul mates?

Chapter - 25

Why do we sleep?

Why do we sleep? Through ages, as man sought to gain more time awake, the need for sleep has remained a curiosity. It is a popular belief that sleep gives the body a chance to recuperate from the day's activities but in reality, the amount of energy saved by sleeping eight hours is about 50 kcal, just about equivalent to the amount of energy present in a piece of toast.

For a long time it was believed that sleep was a state of inactivity that we needed for rest but now it has been clear that there are nerve cells in our brain which fire 5-10 times more frequently during certain stages of sleep than during wakefulness. Lack of sleep has serious effects on the ability of to function. Grogginess, irritability and loss in concentration are some common effects of after just one night without sleep. With continued lack of sufficient sleep, the part of the brain that controls language, memory and sense of time is severally affected. Researches show that Seventen hours of sustained wakefulness leads to a decrease in performance equivalent to a blood alcohol level of 0.05 Percent (about two glasses of wine).

Biologists are now studying the selective pressures that the environment must have cast upon organisms which might have led to primitive sleep. It is now becoming clear that the evolutionary progression towards primitive sleep began as animals with relatively simple lifestyles evolved detailed focal vision (the ability to see a complex scene). As animals acquired vision they engaged in many new activities including fast-ranging movements and rapid actions and responses. In this new transformed lifestyle the maintenance of increasing number of memories for the long term became crucial, such as, memories of locations, predators, regions of food availability etc.

The ability of detailed focal vision created a need for enormous amount of neural processing, vastly more than any other sense, putting great pressure on some regions of the brain. It was increasingly difficult for the brain's processing capabilities to keep up with new information coming through vision and at the same time consolidating and reinforcing long-term memories. Accordingly, the selective pressure for primitive sleep probably was the need for creating a condition in which the brain could perform its functions without interference from outside pressures.

Thus primitive sleep evolved as an evolutionary adaptation to help processing of information by the brain during a portion of the 24 hour cycle. As evolution progressed, the process of sleep became complex and the phases of REM (Rapid Eye Movement) and NREM (Non Rapid Eye Movement) sleep evolved with the advent of warm-bloodedness. Key adaptive changes that accompanied the advent of sleep were eyelids becoming opaque and the ability to close them.

It is likely that the earliest vertebrate sleep occurred in fishes. Among the fishes that show sleep are bony fishes (teleosts) that occupy coral complex reef habitats. Teleosts date back about 235 million years to the Triassic period. Earliest marine forms to exhibit sleep include reef sharks dating back to Ordovician period about 450 million years ago.

Sleeping is not a continuous process of being unconscious for a certain period. In 1950, American physiologists E. Aserinsky and N.Kleitman reported that during each night, we go to through stages of two types of sleep that alternate with each other: Rapid Eye Movement (REM) and Non Rapid Eye Movement (NREM) sleep, so named because of characteristic movement of eyes during sleep.

The amount of the sleep varies significantly with age and even between individuals. A newborn baby sleeps for nearly 17 to 18 hours a day, spending nearly half of that time in REM sleep. Both REM and NREM sleep decreases with age. Children sleep between 10 and 12 hours a day, spending 30 Percent of that time in REM sleep. The average young adult seems to need about 7.75 hours of sleep per night to function optimally during waking hours however some people sleep just Five hours a night. The elderly spend less time in deep NREM sleep, and their sleep is more easily interrupted.

The duration of sleep also varies across animal species. Factors that affect the duration of sleep include the level of development at birth and the size of an animal. Small animals tend to spend more in REM sleep. Modern lifestyle has heavily encroached upon the biological state of sleep and its importance in our lives. 'Artificial Light at Night; is a new concept which is being used to study the role of exposure to light during the night.

Many of the modern day diseases including that of heart, hypertension, cancers and other degenerative conditions have their genesis to altered sleep patterns. Although the earth;s rotation is still as it was for centuries, our perception of night and day has indeed blurred. In this new neon-age, the evolutionary conserved natural sleep has indeed become a luxury.